The SG Story

Dr. Allen Smith

Copyright © 2019 Dr. Allen Smith

All rights reserved.

ISBN: **9781076301376**

DEDICATION

This book is dedicated to three people who love the Southern Gospel Music industry as much as I do; Donna Brock Strong, Brenda Brock Messaros (Hearts of Faith), and Bev McCann. Thank you for the times you jumped in to help with the Diamond Awards when my family could not be there

THE SGN SCOOPS STORY

CONTENTS

1	November 4, 1951	Pg 6
2	The Early Years	Pg 8
3	Salvation and Being Called To Preach	Pg 10
4	Marriage and Children	Pg 15
5	Southern Gospel Radio	Pg 18
6	God Speaks About Magazine	Pg 20
7	Birth of a Magazine	Pg 22
8	Creation of SGN Scoops	Pg 24
9	The Diamond Awards	Pg 26
10	People and Groups	Pg 30
11	Going Digital	Pg 32
12	Failing Health	Pg 33
13	Sale of SGN Scoops and Diamond Awards	Pg 35

ACKNOWLEDGMENTS

First and foremost I would like to thank God for His guidance in putting this book together. I could never have done this without the faith I have in Him.

To my friend Lou Hildreth, who went home to be with the Lord soon after I started this project. She was a constant source of advice and inspiration down through the years.

A most heartfelt note of appreciation to my wife and constant companion, Susan Warkentien Smith. Thank you for your patience, encouragement, and support.

FOREWORD
BY ROB PATZ
PUBLISHER OF SGN SCOOPS MAGAZINE

Dr. Allen Smith has been a great friend to me. I have known him for many years and always appreciated his direct manner and humility of spirit. He has proved to be a loyal brother in Christ and a fountain of good advice.

Allen has been a mentor to me and made the transition of the Magazine ownership smooth. He has always been a visionary with a love and knowledge of gospel music that is unmatched in our field. His publication reflected that vision and understanding.

It was with the presentiment of receiving a torch to hold with dignity and care, that I accepted the legacy of SGN Scoops and the Diamond Awards. I hope that God will allow me to hold what he has passed to me with suitable discernment until I am required to pass it along again.

I have been graced with an excellent team, who work with me to build upon the excellent publication that Allen began years ago. Many of them also are acquainted with Dr. Smith and understand that they are carrying on a legacy of informed, intriguing gospel music news, as well as an awards program that is as unique as it is respected.

Allen has a terrific story to tell and I'm so glad he is sharing it with everyone. This man has been responsible for innovation in the world of gospel music news. God has blessed him richly and guided him along a singular path toward an excellent goal.

Thank you, Allen, from myself and all of us who have benefited from everything you have done in your lifetime.

THE SGN SCOOPS STORY

INTRODUCTION

It has been my heart's desire to write this book for several years. Many people have even approached me and asked me to make such a volume available. Quite frankly, I just did not know where to begin. To me, publishing SGN Scoops was a calling from God. As such, I poured my entire heart into it. This book will address that, and more.

I have spent much prayer and time seeking God on exactly how He wanted me to approach this task. Since I have been a minister of the Gospel of Jesus Christ for over 50 years, this is the way I approach everything I do. His direction means everything to me.

A few nights ago, the Spirit of God began to deal with my heart. In doing so, He laid everything out so simply. For the first time, this task which seemed like an insurmountable mountain, suddenly vanished (Matthew 17:20). The vision I had for this book became so clear and so easy.

I was instructed to start in the beginning. But that is not the day I founded SGN Scoops. He meant MY beginning. You see, God had planned this all before I was even born. He started to prepare me at birth for this great work (Jeremiah 1:5). You see, He does not call you to do anything without first preparing a way for the task to be accomplished (Deuteronomy 31:8 & Philippians 2:13).

So, explaining everything to you about SGN Scoops without telling you about how God prepared me for this important work would only be telling you part of the story. God does not want me to leave anything out. Thus, this work will also be an autobiography of sorts. As you read this work, please remember that as God prepared me to be the founder and publisher of SGN Scoops, He will also prepare you for the work He has called you to do.

THE SGN SCOOPS STORY

1 NOVEMBER 4, 1951

It had been a cold day, colder than everyone was used to for this time of year. A small family was gathered together inside their tiny homestead house just a few miles from the little town of Neoga, Illinois. Two little girls waited outside their parent's bedroom door. One was a little girl with red hair who was 12 years old. The other was a brunette that was 18 months younger. It was past their bedtime, but that was alright, for something special was about to happen.

Dr. L.E. Massie had been there for a while now. He was there to deliver a new brother or sister. The girls were excited, but also worried. You see, they had three siblings younger than themselves who had not lived very long after birth. They were hoping that this would be different.

It was almost midnight, how much longer would it be before the baby was born? Suddenly the girls heard a commotion on the other side of the door. Something was happening, but what was it? Then, like magic, they heard the cry of a little baby! It was 11:54 p.m. and the baby was finally here. The question now was "is it a boy or a girl?"

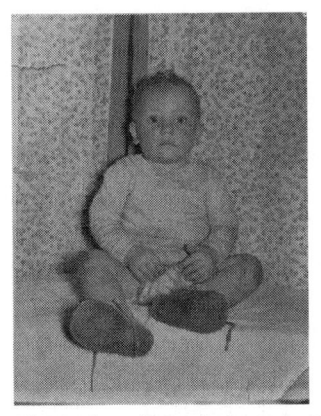

The two girls could hear someone rushing toward the door. It flew open, and their Daddy appeared. "It's a boy", he exclaimed in his excitement. But then, the girls heard something that was not exciting. They heard that someone had to go to the hospital right away. "Is something wrong with my baby brother?" they both thought.

Then they heard that their Mother needed to go to the hospital. She was having problems with her after birth. The tiny little boy was fine, he just needed a name. But their parents had thought of everything. The little boy was to be named after two uncles in California. One was Raymond, and the other was Allen. So, his official name was Raymond Allen Smith, but he was to be called by his middle name, Allen.

So, right after birth, little Allen was wrapped up and given to his sisters to hold and take care of, while their mother was taken to a hospital several miles away. The family was poor, but there was plenty of love to go around. Although this little family did not know Jesus, God's plan was already working. The baby was safe and healthy, and we will explain more in the next chapter.

2 THE EARLY YEARS

Life was not easy for the Smith family as the father of this little household was an alcoholic. For meals, they often ate fried potatoes, beans, and milk gravy. For a change, Mom Smith would sometimes whip up some chocolate gravy for little Allen.

When he was five years old, Mom Smith began taking Allen to church. The church she chose was the First Christian Church in Neoga, Illinois. This was a large brick building which was built in 1925. There are four things that are remembered about this experience. First, at five years old, this was the first time Allen had ever been in a church. Secondly, communion was served every week. Third, the pastor always stood outside the door at the top of the steps to greet people and shake hands with them as they left the service.

The fourth thing to be remembered was a message the pastor preached. Remember, Allen was only five years old at the time. This message was attention-getting, for it used an important visual aid! That morning, the pastor preached on the Crucifixion. When speaking about Jesus being nailed to the cross, the pastor held up a large nail. He shook that nail and brought attention to it.

They only attended that church for a few weeks. Allen did not accept Jesus as his savior at that time. He simply did not understand all of that. But Allen never forgot that message! It simply stuck with him. God never let him forget it. God at this early age was preparing Allen for exciting things that would take place at later times in his life.

Oddly enough, Allen's early preparation did not end with the First Christian Church. He can also remember his parents watching Evangelist Oral Roberts on television. This was during Brother Roberts' tent meeting days. He would preach and he would also lay hands on people while praying for them. This was Allen's first introduction to the Pentecostal belief. This would also stay with Allen through the years. God would also use this experience later during Allen's life. We do not always understand God's way, but looking back, we can see God's hand moving in our lives.

3 SALVATION AND BEING CALLED TO PREACH

Time would pass by, and Allen would not attend church again for several years. His mom and Dad would end up getting a divorce when he was about ten. Allen would live with his dad for a while, and then with his mother. When he was twelve, Allen and his mother would start living in Charleston, Illinois. His two married sisters lived in the same area. Allen's sisters invited them to visit the church they attended.

This church was North Union Separate Baptist Church, located a few miles outside of Charleston. The pastor's name was Jimmy Heath. This was a nice little country church. It wasn't long until Allen's mother gave her heart to the Lord. Shortly after, on a Sunday morning Pastor heath gave an invitation to accept Jesus Christ as Savior.

Allen remembered back to that time when he was just five years old. In his mind, he could still see that huge nail. He could still hear that message on the Crucifixion. He could hear the Lord speaking to his heart saying "I did this for you!" Allen didn't waste any time. He got up from his seat in the back of the church and ran down to the altar. It was then and there, that Allen surrendered his life to Jesus Christ.

Allen was happy in this little church. As pastor Heath took him under his wing, Allen began to learn more and more about the Bible. He even became the youth leader in the church, and occasionally taught the Wednesday evening Bible study. Then one Sunday morning, during a message, Pastor Heath made a statement that was very profound to Allen. That statement was, "We need to get a hold of what the Pentecostals have."

Remembering back to when he was able to watch Evangelist Oral Roberts when he was younger, Allen made the decision that this was also something that needed to be remembered. He could already see the hand of God in his life and could not wait to see what else God had in store for him.

Allen did not have to wait long, for, in a few short months, God moved again in his life. It happened on a Sunday afternoon. To be more specific, it was a Fifth Sunday afternoon. You see, every month that had five Sundays in it, the association of churches that North Union Separate Baptist Church was a part of, would have a community Gospel singing. It was at one of those Gospel singings that Allen heard the voice of God speaking to him. It was very clear, and he had no doubts about it. God specifically called him to preach the Gospel of Jesus Christ.

Allen took this call to heart and had an even greater desire to read and study God's word. He volunteered to do even more things in the church. It was unknown to him at this time, but it would be three more years down the road before he would preach his first sermon. But Allen was happy knowing that he was within God's will.

It wasn't long until Allen's Mom met a Christian man she liked, and they were married in a very short time. His name was Franklin Romano. Frank as everyone called him, was a very good man, and Allen grew to like him very much. It was time to change churches though. Frank attended the First General Baptist Church in Mattoon, Illinois. This was a nice church, and once again, Allen grew very close to his new pastor. After a few months though, things in the church began to change. Those changes hurt a lot of people, and soon, several families left the church. Among those families was Allen, his Mom and his step-dad, Frank.

By this time, Allen was 15 years old and wondered about what church they would attend next. Frank came up with the answer. He had a friend named Rev. Earl Scott who pastored a small Pentecostal church in Mattoon, Illinois. This was really interesting to Allen as he remembered back to the time when he was a child and watched the Oral Roberts programming. He could also remember the words of his former pastor, Jimmy Heath when he said, "We need to get a hold of what the Pentecostals have." Allen was not exactly sure what Pastor Heath meant, but he looked forward to finding out.

The name of the church was House of Prayer Tabernacle. It was different from the other church buildings Allen attended. It was actually a house that was modified so there was a room large enough for a small auditorium. The services were also different than Allen was used to. The people here weren't quiet. They would shout out "Amen," or "Praise the Lord". In addition, they would clap their hands during many songs, and they would also lift up their hands while praising the Lord.

The pastor also preached about the Baptism of the Holy Ghost with the evidence of speaking in other tongues. Allen had never heard this preached before, but it was in the Bible (Acts 10:44-48), and He believed every word in the Bible. It was not long, until Allen and his parents all received the Baptism of the Holy Ghost with the evidence of speaking with other tongues as the Spirit gave them utterance. Allen thought' "Surely this is what Pastor Heath had been speaking about!"

It was during a Wednesday night service that God began to remind Allen that He had called him to preach the Gospel of Jesus Christ. Allen decided to talk to his Pastor about it after service. That is what he did, just as soon as service was over. To his surprise, Frank was waiting for the Pastor also. It seems that he also had been called by God to preach the Gospel. Among other things, the Pastor told them the church had a revival coming up before long during Easter week. It was a revival where different ministers in the church would preach each night. Allen and another young minister would get to preach on Good Friday evening.

Easter week finally came. The service each night went very well. Finally, Good Friday arrived! Allen wanted to remember this date. It was Good Friday, March 24, 1967. He stayed busy that day by praying and studying for his first message. When he got to church that night, Allen found out he would be the last one of the two young ministers to preach. That meant giving the Altar Call that night would be left up to him. As the first minister got up to preach, Allen was getting nervous. The first minister soon sat down, he had only preached for about two minutes. Allen did not have much time to think, as he got up to take his position behind the sacred desk.

Allen read his scripture and then began to speak. He was soon finished. He had only spoken about two minutes himself. It was time for the Altar Call, so Allen invited people to come to the altar that night. Soon the altars were full of people seeking God. Allen learned a very valuable lesson that night. It was not how long one preached, it was whether or not the anointing of God was there. It certainly was that night, as proven by all the people who came to the altar to seek God for their lives.

Allen continued to work and preach in the House of Prayer Tabernacle. Among other things, he served as Youth Leader for the church. He also started and maintained a weekly church newsletter. This was his first time publishing anything. He enjoyed doing it, and the people of the church liked it too. Little did Allen ever dream that he would one day publish a popular Southern Gospel magazine.

Allen enjoyed his time in High School. He attended all four years at Charleston High School in Charleston, Illinois. He made it a point to carry his Bible to school every day. This was an important time in his life, for he learned two important things in high school, that God would use at a later date.

Allen was not a popular student, even though he had plenty of friends. He did not participate in any of the sports programs. He did enjoy working in the school library, so he could do as much research as he desired. He also enjoyed being a member of the projection club. This gave him the responsibility of showing films in different classes.

Today, Allen would be called a geek. He didn't care, he was enjoying life and enjoying being a child of Jesus Christ. One of the classes he took, was Speech. To his astonishment, he found out that while he was preaching, he was already using most of the "tactics" he was learning about making speeches. God is a wonderful teacher.

For his Junior year, one of the classes he signed up for was personal typing which was a one-semester course. To his surprise, Allen ended up in Typing 1, a one year course. Mind you, this was on old fashion nonelectric typewriters. He had no idea why he needed this much typing! But God knew because He knows the end from the beginning. God knew, that computers were coming in a few years down the road, even though Allen did not know.

We must also share with you about Allen's senior year English class. His teacher was Pierce Pickens who also taught a Journalism class. Now, Allen did not take the school's Journalism class, but he was able to learn things about journalism in English class. You see, Mr. Pickens often shared things about journalism during his Senior English class. Allen remembered these things and would use them many years down the road.

Allen graduated from high school when he was 17 years old in May of 1969. His desire was to work for the Lord by becoming a full-time evangelist. He had his own car, which was a 1965 Ford Custom four-door sedan. He was ready to go.

4 MARRIAGE AND CHILDREN

Allen's first revival was held in Joliet, Illinois. It was preached for two weeks in a little church pastored by Rev. Wanda Spenard. The Holy Ghost moved in these services, and souls were added to the Kingdom of God. Allen continued to be excited about what God was doing in his life. He enjoyed being in the will of God.

Once the revival in Joliet was over, Allen headed toward St. Louis, Missouri. There was a little storefront church at Folsom and 39th Street that had booked him for a revival. This church was pastored by Rev. Stella Hofstetter. Once again, the Spirit of God moved during this revival, with souls accepting Jesus Christ as Savior. This revival also lasted for two weeks.

Something unexpected happened on the Saturday night before the revival ended. As Allen went to bed that night, God began to speak to him. God was speaking to him about marrying a girl in the church. He had known this girl for a couple of years from church camp. The problem was, that he already had a girlfriend that he was serious about. For this reason, he told God no.

Allen argued with God all night long that night. Finally, in the early morning hours the next day he said yes to God. It was now Sunday, and the revival was scheduled to end that night. That afternoon a water baptism was scheduled to baptize those who had been saved during the revival. Allen understood from his discussion with God that he was to ask Sharon Ann Tucker to ride back from the Baptism with him. It was during this time that he would propose.

Before the Baptism, Allen looked up Sharon's mother and asked for her permission to ask Sharon to marry him. Sharon's Dad was not in church at that time, so Allen could not speak to him. Sharon's mother told him she gave her permission. Things were all set, now it was time for the water baptism. Several people were baptized that day as Allen and Rev. Hofstetter worked together to do the baptizing.

Afterward, Allen asked Sharon to ride back to the church with him. She agreed to, and they made their way back to the church. They parked near the church and began to talk. A few minutes later Sharon's sister came knocking on the car window and asked, "Has he asked you yet?" This happened 3 or 4 times as Allen and Sharon continued to talk. Finally, Allen worked up the courage and popped the question. Without any hesitation, Sharon said, "Yes!" God had worked on both ends, just as he always does!

Immediately the young couple started making plans for their wedding. It was to be put together as quickly as possible. The date of October 4, 1969, was chosen. That was only two weeks away. It was also just one month before Allen's 18th birthday. A lot of work had to be done in a very short time. However, it all came together, a full-fledged church wedding complete with bridesmaids, groomsmen, and a minister. The minister was Rev. Arlene Rayl of St. Louis, a friend of both the bride and groom.

This was during the time of the Vietnam War, and the military draft. So, when Allen turned 18, he was required to register for the draft. He registered and was classified 1-A. That means he was eligible to be drafted into the armed services of the United States. He also had a low number in the draft lottery which meant he was on the early list to be drafted. Thankfully, Sharon became pregnant in just a few months. When this was reported to the draft board, they gave him a deferment. This meant Allen was no longer eligible for the draft. This felt good to the young couple.

In four months Sharon miscarried their baby. This was devastating to the young couple but within a few short months, Sharon was once again with child. Although there were a few complications, Sharon gave birth to a healthy baby girl on March 5, 1971. They named her Tamara Kay Smith. This was a very happy young family.

Allen suddenly remembered that he needed to notify the draft board about the birth of the new baby. Sadly, the draft board was not happy. It seems Allen had failed to notify the draft board about the miscarriage of the first child. Allen soon received a new draft card. Once again, he was classified 1-A, and again he was eligible for the draft. He still had the low lottery number (039), which meant he could be drafted right away.

For some reason, Allen was never drafted. He was not even called in for a physical as everyone else he knew were. The last draft call was on December 7, 1972; and the Vietnam war ended January 27, 1973. To some, this was all done by chance. But Allen knew the truth. God's hand was in all of this. It was God who kept him out of Vietnam! God kept him safe to work for Him.

Once again, Sharon became pregnant. She gave birth to another little girl on May 9, 1974. They named this beautiful little girl Susan Marie Smith. Her birth was just one day before Allen was scheduled to make a missionary journey to the country of Haiti. His stepfather, Rev. Frank Romano went with him. This was a life changing experience for Allen. He was never the same after making that trip.

5 SOUTHERN GOSPEL RADIO

In the early 1990s, Allen worked for a Christian printing company called Cross Printing. When he first started there, Allen was trained to use an electronic phototypesetting machine. In addition to setting the type, he also developed it. Once that was finished, he would work at the light table to paste up work to get everything ready for someone else to burn the plates and print each job. It wasn't long until the print shop updated their equipment to computers, and started using programs like CorelDraw and Serif PagePlus to do all their typesetting. As such, he was taught to use this new equipment also. While working there, Allen designed and set up different newsletters and magazines. Once again, God was preparing him for a work that he would soon be called to do.

During this time, Allen was also pastoring a little country church a few miles from his Home in DeSoto, Missouri. Allen had a flyer to take to the local Southern Gospel radio station, KHAD which was less than a quarter mile from his house. There he met and became friends with Davy Lee and Alan Brown. Whenever Allen's church had an announcement that needed to be made by the radio station, he would go to the station and spend time with Davy Lee and Alan Brown.

Then in 1995, he was asked to fill a Saturday afternoon Shift at the station. This thrilled Allen because he loved Southern Gospel music. It wasn't long until he was also asked to take a few evening shifts during the week. One of Allen's favorite syndicated programs to play was "Southern Styles" by Rob Patz. It is here that Allen became acquainted with Southern Gospel publications like the Singing News Magazine, The Gospel Voice Magazine, and the U.S. Gospel News. There were also a few regional Southern Gospel newspapers Allen was aware of and received.

This was a wonderful year for Allen, but sadly it did not last. On a Saturday afternoon, he went up to the radio station, and the door was not only locked, but his key would no longer work. The station had been repossessed and closed down. Allen's short radio career was now over. As he made his way home, he began to wonder what direction the Lord would lead him in now.

6 GOD SPEAKS ABOUT MAGAZINE

Allen did not have to wait long as he could hear a still small voice tell him to start a Southern Gospel magazine. The problem was though he was not sure it was the voice of the Lord speaking to him. One day he received a call from Alan Brown. He was now at a brand new Southern Gospel radio station in Marble Hill, Missouri, KMHM 104.1 FM. Alan Brown invited him down to visit. Within a couple of days, Allen made his way to Marble Hill. There he met with Station Manager Rick Jones and General Manager Doug Apple.

After spending time with Alan Brown, Allen found out that KMHM also published a monthly Southern Gospel newspaper. He was told they just started publishing the paper and asked him if he could help them distribute it. Allen thought, "Maybe this is what the Lord wants me to do. But, that is not all they asked him to do. He was given a tape recorder and asked to interview Southern Gospel singers at concerts.

This worked well for several months, but soon the newspapers were no longer available to Allen. He could once again hear the voice of the Lord speaking to him to start a Southern Gospel magazine. Then he was told about another Southern Gospel Newspaper and went to see the publisher. This was a much nicer and more informative paper. Right away, the publisher asked for his help.

Believing this was what the Lord wanted him to do, Allen gladly said yes, and started to work. This went on for about three months, and he was very happy with what he was doing. Then all of a sudden Allen received word that this newspaper had run out of money and closed down. Allen sat down and began to wonder about all this. Then he once again heard the voice of the Lord speaking to him. This time he knew for sure this was the voice of the Lord, and he knew exactly what God wanted him to do. "Now are you ready to do what I want you to do?" was the question the Lord asked Allen that day!

7 BIRTH OF A MAGAZINE

Allen pondered what God had spoken to his heart. He was pastoring a little church in Potosi, Missouri named Full-Gospel Tabernacle. For several months now, the church had been sponsoring Southern Gospel concerts in the Potosi area. They had one coming up in a few weeks. In fact, it was to be held on Halloween night, Thursday, October 31, 1996. The group scheduled was The Kingsmen. "This would be a great time to introduce the new magazine," Allen thought.

So he started to work on the first issue of the magazine. He already had the software he needed on his computer. He knew that Cross Printing would print it for him. He would then fold it and staple it together. He had to decide the number of pages to start out with. That was an easy decision. He would start out with 8 pages. That meant that each magazine would take 2 sheets of 11 X 17 paper.

The next thing that needed to be done was to come up with a name for the new publication. Since the new magazine was being published in the state of Missouri, and it would contain Southern Gospel news, it should be called "Missouri Southern Gospel News". Things were working out quite nicely, but Allen was not finished yet. He had to decide how many copies he would need for the first issue. Based on the size of the audience that was expected for the concert, it was decided to print 200 copies.

The next step was to go to Cross Printing and give them all the information they needed to give him a quote for the price of printing. Allen did this and waited a few days to receive the quote. Once he received the quote, the next step was to figure out how many ads he would need to sell in order to get the magazine printed. Now, the hard work had to be done. Allen had to go out and sell ads in Potosi and the Leadbelt area of Missouri to sell ads to businesses.

First, Allen designed a sample magazine which showed all of the ad sizes that were available. He then designed the front cover of the magazine so prospective advertisers could see that The Kingsmen would be on the cover. Allen then started to work. It took a few days, but finally, enough ads were sold to have the magazine printed. All Allen needed to do now was to decide all the material that would be in the magazine, and design it all, including the ads.

Finally, the job was finished and the masters were taken to Cross Printing for printing. It took about a week for the printing to be finished. Allen, his wife Sharon, his daughters Tammy and Suzy, his sons-in-law Jeff and Clifton worked to collate and fold the magazine. Allen then went back to Cross Printing and used their saddle stapler to staple each magazine together.

Now it was time for the big night. The Kingsmen showed up. The crowd showed up. The magazines were introduced and passed out. The crowd excitedly accepted the new magazine. The entire concert was a great success. Allen went home as a very happy man since God had once again blessed him for being in His will.

8 CREATION OF SGN SCOOPS

The name Missouri Southern Gospel News lasted for about 3 months. The popularity of the new magazine caused it to explode out of the state of Missouri. When this happened, it was quickly decided to drop Missouri from the name of the magazine. Now, it was simply called Southern Gospel News. Allen soon realized since we were in the electronic age, that a new source for Southern Gospel information needed to be started. That brand new source of information was a weekly Email newsletter.

This new weekly publication was named SGN Scoops. The letters "SGN" was an acronym for Southern Gospel News. The word "Scoops" indicated that the news being published was being provided accurately and quicker than anyone else did. This new publication envisioned by Allen Smith quickly became popular with everyone, including not only fans but everyone in the industry. It was so popular that its subscriptions quickly outgrew the original magazine.

Shortly after this, Allen received an email from a young lady from Florida. Her name was Jennifer Campbell. She wanted to become a writer for the magazine. She was only 15 years old and attended a Christian school. Allen decided to give her a chance and asked her to submit a sample article. She did and as they say, the rest is history. Jennifer was immediately added as a staff writer and began writing most of the magazines cover stories. If you look at a copy of SGN Scoops Magazine today you will find that Jennifer is still on the staff of writers.

In just a few short months, the popularity of SGN Scoops out-paced the popularity of the magazine. It is very safe to say that the people who had anything to do with Southern Gospel music, whether fans or the Southern Gospel industry were better acquainted with the name SGN Scoops than they were with the name Southern Gospel News. Once again it was decided to change the name of the magazine. The new name was SGN Scoops Magazine.

9 THE DIAMOND AWARDS

In 2002 Allen realized that SGN Scoops needed an awards program. He really did not want to start up a new program. He wanted one that was already established. But, that was something that was impossible! But Allen knew someone who was the master of the impossible! So Allen began to pray. It was just a few days when God began to speak to him. God reminded him about The Diamond Awards that had been produced by The Gospel Voice Magazine.

The Gospel Voice Magazine started The Diamond Awards in 1991. Sadly their last program was in the year 2000. The Gospel Voice closed down their publication in 2001. God reminded Allen that he knew one of the last owners of The Gospel Voice, and instructed Allen to contact him. This meant a trip to the Meramec Music Theatre in Steelville, Missouri. The theatre held a monthly Gospel Music concert, and the man Allen needed to talk to was the MC at the concerts.

Allen was sure to make it to the next Southern Gospel Concert at The Meramec Music Theatre. He looked up Wayne Gott and talked to him about The Diamond Awards. Basically, Mr. Gott stated that he had a partner, and would have to speak to him before a decision could be made. He then told Allen to come to the next month's concert. Allen agreed to do that.

It seemed like that month took forever to come around. But it did, and Allen returned to Meramec Music Theatre. When Allen looked up Mr. Gott, the news was good! SGN Scoops could have The Diamond Awards. It did not cost one thin dime. Once again, God had come through for him. Now it was time to go to work so that The Diamond Awards would be ready for 2003.

So many things needed to be done. The venue was needed for the program. A place needed to be selected to purchase all the awards. MC's would need to be selected. Advertising needed to be done. A sound system must be procured. A voting system needed to be set up. Funds were needed for all of this. Was it even possible to pull it all together in time?

Slowly it all came together. Lamp Music Group agreed to sponsor the first Diamond Awards produced by SGN Scoops. This took care of the venue and the sound system. It was decided to use printed ballots in SGN Scoops, and email votes. Mark Bishop and Kyla Rowland agreed to be the first MCs. A place was selected to purchase all of the awards. Advertising would be sold to pay all necessary expenses. It was also decided that Allen's grandchildren would bring the awards on stage to the presenters.

But this was not all. The Diamond Awards always had 2 special awards. In order to show that this was the same awards program as before, identical awards had to be presented. The two special awards were The Lou Wills Hildreth Award and the Paul Heil Award. So Allen contacted both Paul Heil and Lou Wills Hildreth. They both agreed to continue their respective awards.

The venue that was selected was a hotel in Louisville Kentucky. It was just outside the main gate of the Kentucky Fair and Expo Center. This is where the National Quartet Convention was held at that time. The votes had been tallied, and the guest performers were all set. The day and the hour finally arrived. Allen wearing a tuxedo stepped on The Diamond Awards stage for the first time. There he announced, "Welcome to the 2003 SGN Scoops Diamond Awards."

After an opening prayer, Allen said, "Now let us make this more than an awards program, let's worship God." He then turned the program over to the MCs, Mark Bishop, and Kyla Rowland.

There is no doubt that the first Diamond Awards under the SGN Scoops Banner was a tremendous success. Everyone was excited, but most of all, the Spirit of the Lord was there! To show you an example of what took place that day, I want to give an illustration of an incident that took place that day, that Allen remembers to this day. One of the performing groups that day arrived without their piano player. They went up on stage anyway and explained the situation. Out of the crowd, a small man began to run through the crowd and jumped up on the stage. He sat down at the piano and start playing. That small man was the incomparable Anthony Burger! This set the tone for all future SGN Scoops Diamond Awards.

The prestigious Diamond Awards have a history of over 20 years, recognizing the best in Gospel Music from coast to coast. Many of today's top artists have received Diamond Award nominations and awards, from Doyle Lawson and Quicksilver to the Booth Brothers to the

Hoppers. They were the first Southern Gospel fan-based awards and are still open to everyone, no subscription required. The Diamond Awards have always been pleased to salute Christian artists who strive to use their talent to the best of their ability and to God's glory.

10 PEOPLE AND GROUPS

1969 was a very good year for Allen. As we have already mentioned, He graduated from high school when he was only 17 years old. He got married and even started pastoring his first church. This is also when he first became acquainted with Southern Gospel music. Radio Station KXEN 1010 AM on the dial was blasting Southern Gospel music at 50,000 watts. There he was introduced to many of his favorite groups like The Rambos, The Downings, The Bill Gaither Trio, The Lanny Wolf Trio, The Hemphills, The Happy Goodman Family, The Hinsons, The Sego Brothers and Naomi and many others. It was during this same period of time that Allen became friends with 2 very well-known local groups, Gene Warren and the Glorylanders, and The Singing Loves. Then in the late 1970s, Allen met and became friends with St. Louis' First Family of Gospel Music, The Lesters.

When Allen began interviewing groups for Radio Station KMHM 104.1 FM in Marble Hill, Missouri, he became acquainted with The Kingsmen, The Bishops, Tony Gore & majesty and others. During this time Allen's church was also sponsoring Southern Gospel concerts; and he became acquainted with The Mckameys, The Segoes, The Greenes, and Garry Sheppard.

Once the magazine was started in 1996, things began to change quickly as the internet became available to everyone. Allen also began making annual trips to the National Quartet Convention in Louisville, Kentucky. While there, Allen would take extra copies of SGN Scoops Magazine with him and pass those copies to the groups that were there, as well as the Southern Gospel businesses. People became more acquainted with the magazine, and Allen began to be invited to different NQC events.

Allen quickly became friends with many of the exhibitors at NQC. The one he is still most proud of to this date is the head of Coastal Media Group, Rob Patz. The is the same Rob Patz that had the syndicated radio program "Southern Styles" that Allen played at Radio Station KHAD in DeSoto, Missouri. Rob immediately started distributing copies of SGN Scoops Magazine from his booth at NQC.

It would be easy to list people Allen became friends with at NQC. We will just name a few here; Garry Cohn and Eddie Crook of The Gospel Voice Magazine, Ed and Jeff Harper of The Harper Agency, Beckie Simmons of The Beckie Simmons Agency, Ed and Dottie Leonard of Daywind Music, Paul R. Boden founder and editor of The U.S. Gospel News, and more.

Once The Diamond Awards started up, things really exploded. We have already mentioned Lou Wills Hildreth and Paul Heil. Kyla Rowland and Mark Bishop became the first MC's of The Diamond Awards. Karen Peck Gooch and Johnathan Bond became MCs of The Diamond Awards and friends of Allen, as well. Many of the top name groups performing at The Diamond Awards have been The Hoppers, The Talleys, Karen Peck & New River, The Hoskin Family, The Crabb Family, Dixie Melody Boys, The Issacs, The Florida Boys, The Blackwood Quartet and more.

11 GOING DIGITAL

SGN Scoops was the first to do many things, but the most important was going digital. Allen had thought about it for several years. He researched it for just about as long, but he was just too far ahead of his time. Not even PDF was ready to do what Allen needed to be done. The main problem was the size of the files. But he kept working, he kept trying, then one day, presto it worked!

In 2008 it finally happened! SGN Scoops finally went digital. It was the first magazine of this type to do so. This was perhaps the greatest achievement of the magazine. It was not long until many people were downloading SGN Scoops Digital to their personal computers. The magazine began to grow faster than it ever had before.

12 FAILING HEALTH

On May 24, 2007, Allen's wife Sharon died of Uterine Cancer. This devastated him, he and Sharon had been married just short of 38 years. His daughters Tammy and Suzy helped him as much as they could. One of Allen's problems was he had not been to a doctor in several years. He told his daughters that he would make a doctor's appointment right away. He did so and got in to see a doctor within two weeks of Sharon's burial.

Allen found out right away that he had Type 2 Diabetes with Peripheral Neuropathy. In fact, he had been experiencing both for several years. Allen also found out he had several other problems which were a result of the Diabetes.

It was not long before God began to move in Allen's life again. This time God led him to another helpmate. He would no longer be alone. This woman had spent most of her life on the mission field with her parents in the country of Brazil. Her name was Susan C. Warkentien. They were married on July 12, 2008.

Time continued on and Allen's health continued to gradually get worse. Then in September of 2008, Allen had a stroke and ended up in the hospital. He was only there for a few days, for God touched his body in many ways.

It was not long until Allen needed 2 stints in his heart. He also found out he was in 3rd Stage Kidney disease. Then in 2009, he had another stroke. It seemed that Allen's health was quickly deteriorating. He knew that it would not be long until he would not be able to work on SGN Scoops or take care of The Diamond Awards. He thought back at 2 Southern Gospel Magazines that had to close down. They were the U.S. Gospel News and The Gospel Voice Magazine. The U.S. Gospel News had closed down because its owner had passed away. Allen did not want SGN Scoops to have to close down for any reason, but he was rapidly getting where his body would no longer allow him to keep up the pace he was on.

13 SALE OF SGN SCOOPS AND DIAMOND AWARDS

With his chronic health issues causing him many problems, Allen began to pray. All during his life, God had never failed him. God would not fail him now either. Allen knew he could not work on SGN Scoops much longer. He also knew he would not be able to produce The Diamond Awards much longer. There was no doubt that he had taken both of them every step he could take them. Someone else needed to take them over! Once again, God spoke to Allen's heart, he was to contact his friend Rob Patz to take it over. Coastal Media was already sponsoring The Diamond Awards in Branson, Missouri that year. The awards were only a couple of months away.

Allen called Rob and told him that he wanted to talk to him about something at The Diamond Awards. Allen does not like to talk business over the phone and wanted the discussion to take place in person. Rob's interest was captured, and he did not want to wait. His desire was to find out then and there what Allen wanted. Allen gave in and told Rob he needed to give up SGN Scoops and The Diamond Awards because of His health. He also told Rob that while praying about the matter, God had told him to contact Rob Patz. In just a few short minutes God had his way with both parties.

The deal was made there on the phone. There was no paperwork made up, there was no up-front money. Just two people doing what God wanted them to do. That year Allen and Rob Co-produced the SGN Scoops Diamond Awards. How Rob took both SGN Scoops and The SGN Scoops Diamond Awards to even greater heights is another story altogether!

ABOUT THE AUTHOR

Dr. Allen Smith was born in the little town of Neoga, IL in 1951. He was saved at the early age of 12 years and started preaching when he was just 15. He has been preaching and teaching now for 52 years. He has been a pastor for over 30 years of that time. Dr. Smith has been a featured speaker at camp-meetings and conventions down through the years. In addition, he spent 3 years as president of International Bible College and Seminary in DeSoto, Missouri, where he authored 9 different syllabi for the Seminary.

Dr. Smith presently holds a Master's Degree in Religious Education, a Doctor of Divinity Degree, and a Doctor of Theology Degree and has published several articles, in nationwide religious publications, and has published several books which have been listed in the back of this book.

From October of 1996 until July of 2009, Dr. Smith published a nationwide Southern Gospel news magazine called SGN Scoops Digital. He is currently the founder and President of Lighthouse International Ministries which is a missionary outreach and publishing ministry.

IF YOU WOULD LIKE TO BE SAVED

Pray This Prayer With Your Whole Heart

Dear Heavenly Father, I realize that I have broken your laws and I am a sinner. I understand that my sin has separated me from you. I am sorry and I ask you to forgive me. I accept the fact that your son Jesus Christ died for me, was resurrected, and is alive today and hears my prayers. I now open my heart and invite Jesus in to become my Lord and Saviour. I give Him control and ask that He would rule and reign in my heart so that His perfect will would be accomplished in my life. In Jesus name, I pray. Amen.

Congratulations!

If you prayed this prayer in all sincerity, you are now a Child of God. But, there are a few things that you need to do to follow up on your commitment to the Lord.

(1) **Get baptized (full immersion) in water as commanded by Jesus**

(2) **Tell someone else about your new faith in Jesus**

(3) Spend time with God each day through prayer and Bible reading

(4) Seek fellowship with other followers of Jesus

So that we might rejoice with you, we invite you to contact us and

Let us know about the decision you made!

You may contact Dr. Smith at dr.allensmith.author@gmail.com

One Last Thing....

Thank you so much for reading this book. You have no idea how much it means to me. I hope you have been able to enjoy "The SGN Scoops Story", and that you have grown closer to the Lord. If you have enjoyed reading this book, I would deeply appreciate it if you would write a short review on Amazon.com. As you know, reviews are what usually helps a person to make a decision, when they are looking at a book. If you think other people would benefit from the information contained in this book then let them know! You can leave a short review here: http://www.amazon.com/

Also, when you turn the page Amazon will ask you to rate this book and give you the option of sharing your rating via Twitter and Facebook. I would love it if you would rate this book and let your social networking friends know about it! Thanks again for reading.

Dr. Allen Smith

Check Out Dr. Smith's Kindle Books

"Why?" on Amazon.com.

"One Day At A Time" on Amazon.com.

"The Sacrifice" on Amazon.com.

"Porquê?" on Amazon.com.

"The Ultimate Guide To Kindle Publishing Using Microsoft Word" on Amazon.com

"The Unknown Enemy" on Amazon.com

"Daily Manna" on Amazon.com

"Life-Changing Worship Manual" on Amazon.com

Check Dr. Smith's Paperback Books

"Life-Changing Worship Manual" on Amazon.com

"One Day At A Time" on Amazon.com

"The Sacrifice" on Amazon.com

"Why?" on Amazon.com

"Daily Manna" on Amazon.com

Check Out Our "Lighthouse Christian Classics

"Heaven" by D.L. Moody on Amazon.com

"Sinners In The Hands Of An Angry God" by Jonathan Edwards on Amazon.com

"Ever Increasing Faith by Smith Wigglesworth on Amazon.com

"Foxes Book Of Martyrs" by John Foxe on Amazon.com

"The Life Of Dwight L. Moody" by William R. Moody on Amazon.com

"Faith That Prevails" by Smith Wigglesworth on Amazon.com

Keep Up-To-Date With Dr. Smith

You may contact Dr. Smith at dr.allensmith.author@gmail.com

Made in the USA
Columbia, SC
23 February 2020